BASIC FINGERPICKING
A GUIDE TO FINGERPICKING IN ALL STYLES

T0048228

INTRODUCTION

Fingerpicking guitar has always been an essential part of rock, pop, blues, country, folk, jazz, and classical music. As Ry Cooder once said, "We have this incredibly, complicated tool: the hand. Why reduce it to a tiny plastic triangle?"

A fingerpicker can blend with a band or be a self-contained soloist. If you fingerpick well, you can be rhythm, bass, and lead guitar rolled into one. That's why so many contemporary singer/songwriters fingerpick: it beats hiring a band — a fingerpicked guitar can sound like a whole orchestra.

This book introduces you to a whole range of fingerpicking styles, with an emphasis on contemporary sounds. It's for beginners or guitarists who already play, but not with their fingers. Using music, tablature, and an accompanying recording, it teaches you how to fingerpick back-up to many rhythmic grooves, and how to solo in several keys.

Fingerpicking is one of the most satisfying, complete ways to play guitar, so let's tune up and get started...

Fred Sokolow

PLAYBACK+
Speed • Pitch • Balance • Loop

To access audio visit:
www.halleonard.com/mylibrary

Enter Code
8872-5147-1091-6247

ISBN 978-0-7935-8072-9

HAL•LEONARD®
CORPORATION

7777 W. BLUEMOUND RD. P.O. BOX 13819 MILWAUKEE, WI 53213

Visit Hal Leonard Online at
www.halleonard.com

CONTENTS

LISTENING SUGGESTIONS

You can improve your fingerpicking by listening to and imitating other players. Besides the pop songwriters/pickers mentioned in this book, here are some blues, country, rock and pop players who bear listening to:

Blues

For *raggy blues*, which features an alternating thumb/bass, listen to "first generation" blues pickers:

Mississippi John Hurt, Elizabeth Cotten, Blind Blake, Blind Boy Fuller, Furry Lewis, Blind Willie McTell, Reverend Gary Davis, Jesse Fuller, Skip James, Tampa Red, Lonnie Johnson.

Texas-style players, or pickers who usually play a monotone thumb/bass, include:

Mance Lipscomb, Lightnin' Hopkins, Big Bill Broonzy, Brownie McGhee, Blind Lemon Jefferson, Huddie Ledbetter (Leadbelly).

Country

Fingerpicking is still an important part of the contemporary country sound. Some players who contributed to the art include:

Merle Travis, Chet Atkins, Jerry Reed, Sam McGee, Doc Watson.

'60s and '70s Folk, Rock and Folk-Rock

These fingerpickers were inspired by the above blues and country legends:

Bob Dylan, Joni Mitchell, Tom Paxton, Joan Baez, Jorma Kaukonen (Jefferson Airplane and Hot Tuna), Paul Simon, the Beatles, Keith Richards (the Rolling Stones), John Fahey, Leo Kottke, Jimmy Page (Led Zeppelin), James Taylor, Lindsey Buckingham (Fleetwood Mac), Eric Clapton.

Other Virtuosi

Doyle Dykes, Michael Hedges, Bert Jansch, Will Ackerman, Laurence Juber, Martin Simpson.

PRELIMINARIES

 ## Tuning Up

Starting from the 6th (heaviest) string, the standard guitar tuning is E, A, D, G, B, E. Once you get an E note from another instrument, pitch pipe or tuning fork, you can use the string-to-string method, below, to tune the other strings:

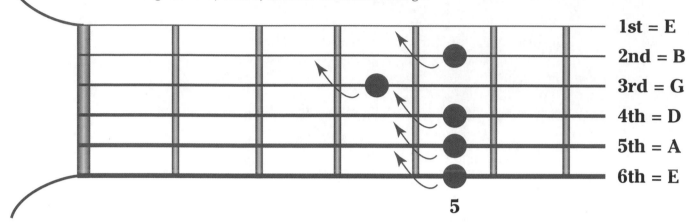

1st = E
2nd = B
3rd = G
4th = D
5th = A
6th = E

5

- • Fret the 6th string at the 5th fret. Tune the 5th string to match the resulting A note.
- • Fret the 5th string at the 5th fret. Tune the 4th string to match the resulting D note.
- • Fret the 4th string at the 5th fret. Tune the 3rd string to match the resulting G note.
- • Fret the 3rd string at the 4th fret. Tune the 2nd string to match the resulting B note.
- • Fret the 2nd string at the 5th fret. Tune the 1st string to match the resulting E note.

How to Read Chord Grids

A *chord grid* is a picture of four or five frets of the guitar's fretboard. The dots show you where to fret (finger) the strings:

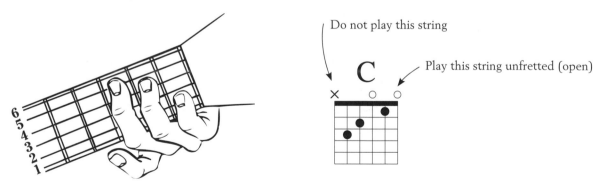

Do not play this string

C

Play this string unfretted (open)

How to Read Tablature

Songs, scales and exercises in this book are written in standard music notation and tablature. The six lines of the tablature staff represent the six guitar strings:

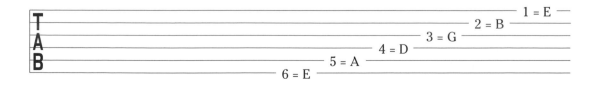

1 = E
2 = B
3 = G
4 = D
5 = A
6 = E

A number on a line tells you which string to play and where to fret it.

This example means
"play the 3rd string on
the 4th fret"

This example means
"play the 4th string
unfretted"

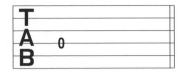

Chords can also be written in tablature:

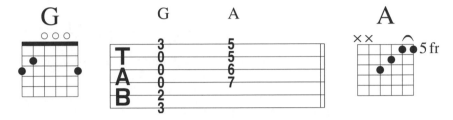

All the details of tablature notation (hammer-ons, slides, etc.) are explained in the *Notation Legend* at the back of this book.

Fingerpicks

Many fingerpicking guitarists wear a thumbpick and fingerpick or two as shown in the illustration below. Most prefer plastic thumbpicks, which come in different sizes, and metal fingerpicks, which you can bend to fit your fingers. You don't *need* fingerpicks, but some players prefer the crisp, bright sound they lend. If you play *hard and loud* on an acoustic, steel-stringed guitar, picks save wear and tear on your fingertips.

Some players prefer to pick with their right-hand fingernails. They may use a nail-hardening polish to protect their nails.

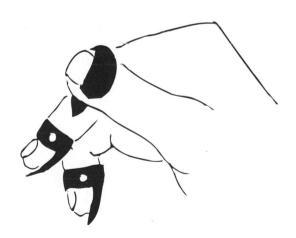

FINGERPICKING BACKUP — THE GROOVES

Most fingerpickers accompany their own singing by playing a repetitious pattern, one they can play without thinking about it. The idea is to keep a steady rhythm, make the chord changes and concentrate on singing. Once you become comfortable with a pattern, you can add runs that connect chords, plus other subtleties.

The patterns and tunes that follow will get you started playing some typical fingerpicking accompaniment for several different grooves:

- Any pattern can be used to create more than one rhythmic feel.

- There are countless ways (patterns) to fingerpick any particular groove. No one way is right or wrong.

- Once you choose a pattern, consistency is important.

- Practice the patterns and tunes that follow by repeating them over and over with a steady rhythm, even if you have to slow them down to keep them flowing smoothly.

The Picking Hand

As early as the 1920s, African-American blues guitarists popularized a fingerpicking style in which the thumb picks alternating bass notes (usually the root and fifth of the chord being played) and the fingers play melody or fill out the rhythm on the treble strings. This style has been the basis for a great deal of blues, country, folk, rock and folk-rock guitar playing. Sometimes it's combined with classic or flamenco techniques. In this blues-based tradition…

- The thumb picks the bass (6th, 5th, 4th and sometimes 3rd) strings.

- The index finger plays the treble strings (the 1st, 2nd and 3rd).

- Many pickers use the middle finger to pick the 1st string.

- The ring and little fingers are used infrequently (see the *Other Tempos and Techniques* chapter for the use of the ring and little fingers).

Since most picking is done with the thumb, index and middle fingers, many players rest their ring and little fingers (or just their little finger) on the guitar below the soundhole, to stabilize their picking hand. This is contrary to classical guitar technique, but nearly all the pioneering blues and country pickers did it, so it has its own tradition, and most people find it helpful.

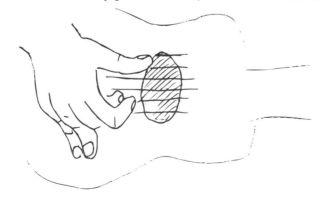

Basic Backup Pattern with Alternating Bass

The three bars below show how the basic backup pattern works. The thumb plays alternating bass notes on the first, second, third and fourth beats of each bar, while the fingers play between those beats. (Note: on the notation staff, the downstemmed notes should be played with the thumb.)

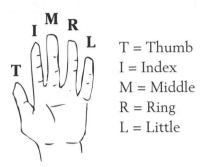

T = Thumb
I = Index
M = Middle
R = Ring
L = Little

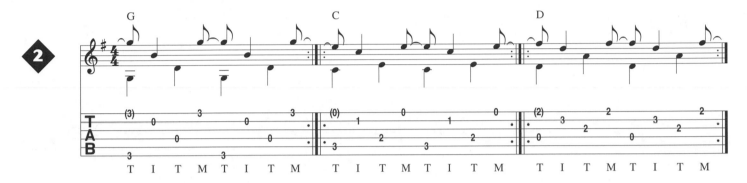

This basic pattern fits several different rhythm grooves. "Bejeweled," which follows, has a shuffle beat feel similar to Jewel's hit song, "Who Will Save Your Soul." This loping rhythmic feel is used in country/pop tunes like Roger Miller's "King of the Road" and Johnny Rivers' "Mountain of Love." The song uses these four chords:

③ BEJEWELED

In Beatles tunes like "Julia," "Happiness Is a Warm Gun" and "Dear Prudence," the Beatles used the basic pattern to create a folky, cut-time groove. It's the same feel immortalized in such folk-pop hits as Bob Dylan's "Don't Think Twice, It's All Right" and Peter Paul and Mary's "Puff the Magic Dragon." "Sixties Folk," which follows, has a typical cut-time groove, and it features a slight variation of the basic pattern:

◆ 4 SIXTIES FOLK

Rock Grooves

The next tune, "Swan Song," has the same fingerpicking pattern as "Bejeweled." In this tune, it creates a rock groove like the one in Suzanne Vega's hit, "My Name Is Louka." A similar "straight-eighths" rock groove is found in songs like Rod Stewart's "Maggie May" "Every Breath You Take" by the Police and the Beatles' "Get Back." The song uses these chords:

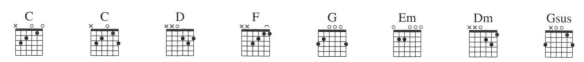

⬥ 5 SWAN SONG

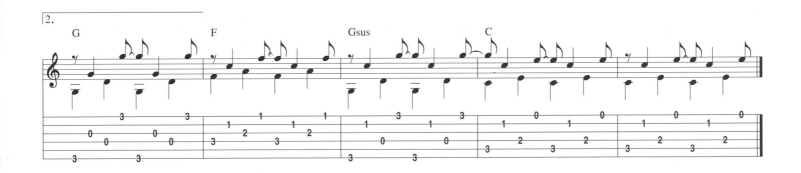

"Bayou Rock" is a "swamp-rock" groove *à la* Creedence Clearwater's "Born on the Bayou." This is very similar to the straight-eighths groove of "Swan Song," above. It's based on a two-bar variation of the basic pattern:

⬥ 6 BAYOU ROCK

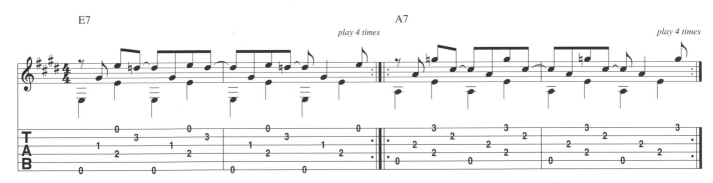

This pattern can also create a rock ballad feel, as in Kenny Rogers' "Lady" or James Taylor's "You've Got a Friend" or Led Zeppelin's "Stairway to Heaven." "Taylor-Made," below, has this groove:

⑦ TAYLOR-MADE

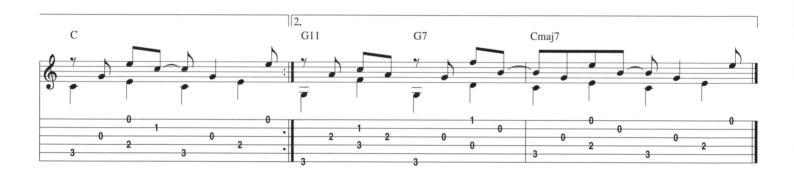

A two-bar variation of the basic pattern makes a good rockabilly groove, suitable for songs like "Blue Suede Shoes" (Carl Perkins, Elvis Presley), Queen's "Crazy Little Thing Called Love" and the Beatles' "All My Loving." "Careless Love" has the same feel:

Two-Bar Pattern

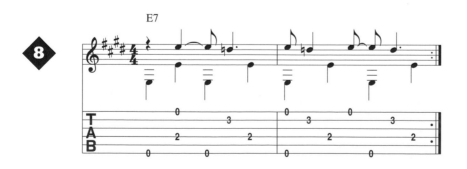

9 CARELESS LOVE

Love,   oh   love, oh care - less love.

Love,   oh   love, oh care - less love.

Love,   oh   love, oh   care - less   love,

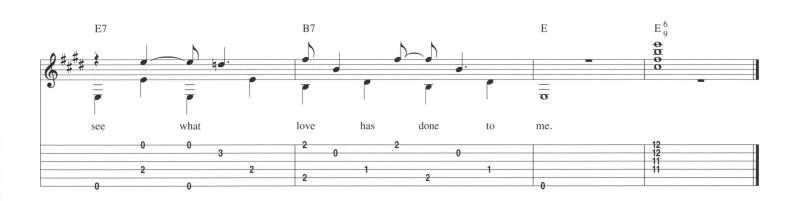

see   what   love   has   done   to   me.

Funky Half-Time Rock Grooves

"Any Flavor" uses a variation of the basic pattern that creates a funky rhythm similar to that of Ani DiFranco's "Thirty-Two Flavors." Tunes with a similar groove include Tina Turner's "What's Love Got To Do With It" and "Love the One You're With" by Crosby, Stills and Nash.

ANY FLAVOR

"Swamp Water," below, has a half-time "swamp-rock" feel like the Doobie Brothers' "Black Water." "After Midnight" (Eric Clapton) and "Wild Thing" (The Troggs, Jimi Hendrix) have a similar groove.

SWAMP WATER

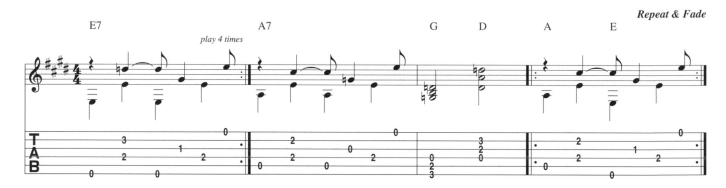

A Half-Time Rock Ballad Groove

"Valentine," below, illustrates how to alter the basic backup pattern to make it fit a half-time rock-ballad feel, such as the groove Sting created in "Shape of My Heart." Marvin Gaye's "What's Going On" and Roberta Flack's "Feel Like Makin' Love" have a similar feel. A two-bar pattern is played throughout:

Here are the chords used in "Valentine":

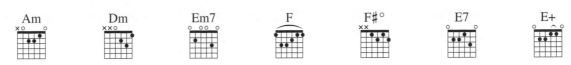

13 ◆ VALENTINE

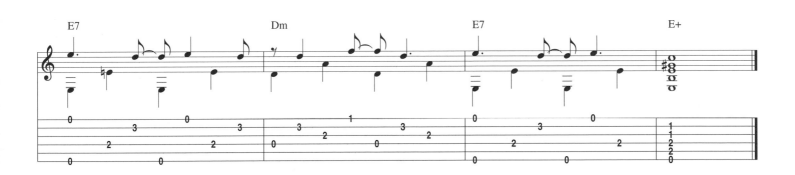

Moving Bass Lines

"Indigo Mood" is a half-time rock ballad with the rhythmic feel the Indigo Girls created in their ballad, "Ghost." Elton John's "Rocket Man" and Lynyrd Skynyrd's "Free Bird" have a similar groove.

The backup includes ascending and descending bass lines, which are created by inversions, chords that do not have their root in the bass. Inversions are written as fractions, with the chord on top and the bass note on the bottom. D/F♯ means: a D chord with F♯ in the bass. Here are the inversions and other chords in "Indigo Mood":

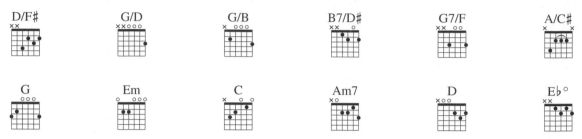

Here's the basic picking pattern for "Indigo Mood":

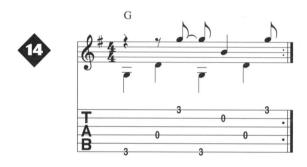

🔷15 INDIGO MOOD

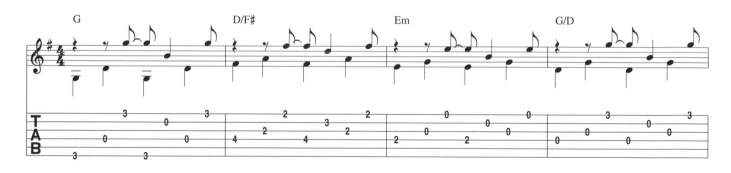

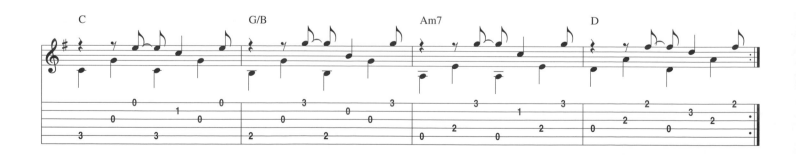

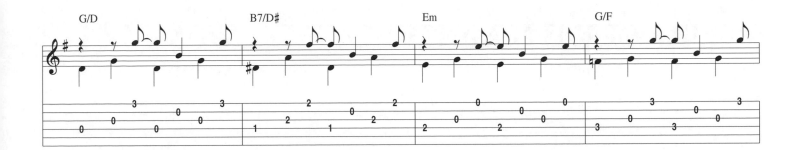

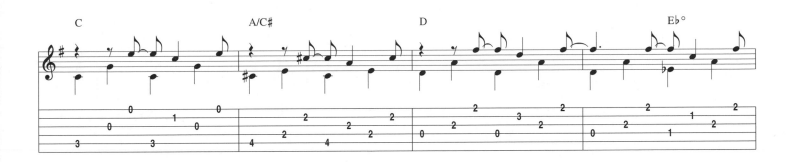

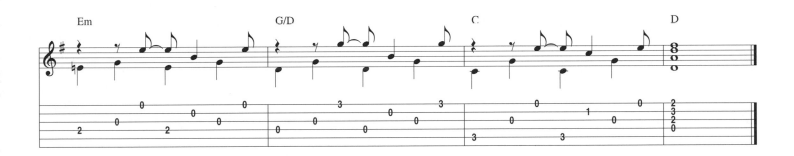

Adding Bass Runs

Bass runs connect one chord to another and often fill a gap in a vocal line. "Blue Nancy" shows how to add them to the basic fingerpicking pattern. It's a country-rock ballad in the style of Nanci Griffith's "Once in a Very Blue Moon." The Eagles "Best of My Love" and James Taylor's "You've Got a Friend" have a similar groove.

16 ◆ BLUE NANCY

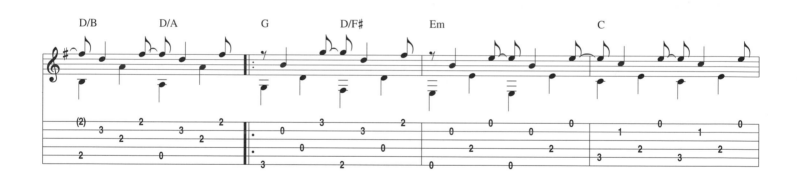

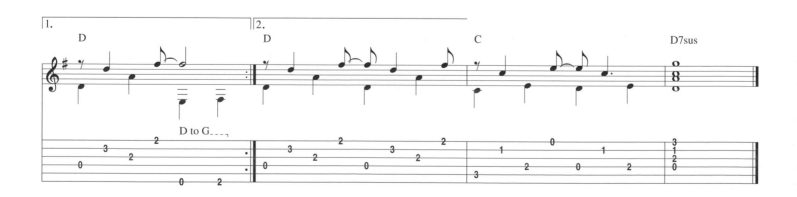

Bass Run Exercise

The following exercise takes you through many bass runs. As you'll hear when playing the exercise, it's okay to stop filling out the rhythm with your fingers during the bass runs.

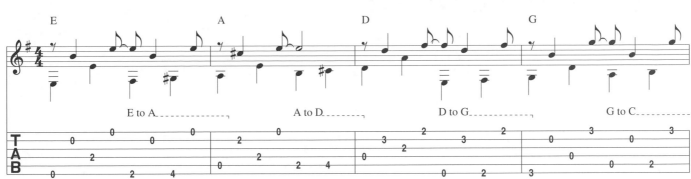

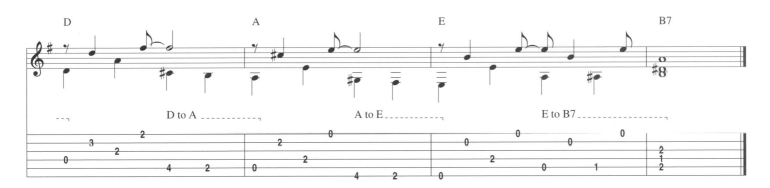

Double Alternating Bass

Alternating between three bass notes, instead of two, adds variety to the basic fingerpicking pattern:

"MacPumpkin" features a double-alternating bass throughout. It has the same feel as Fleetwood Mac's "Landslide" (also recorded by the Smashing Pumpkins) and Kansas' "Dust in the Wind."

◆19 MacPUMPKIN

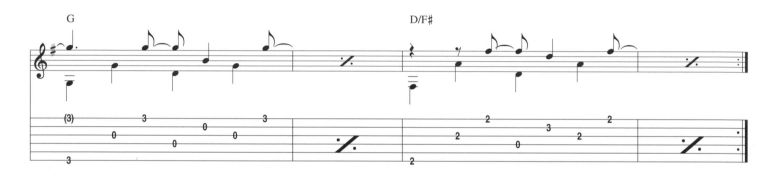

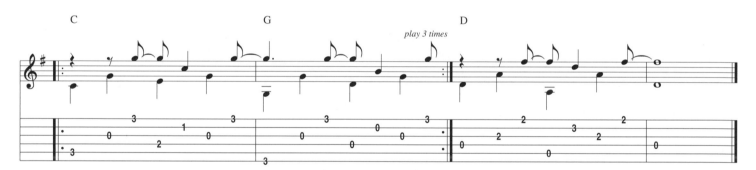

Add-Ons and Drop-Offs

To vary a picking pattern, you can add notes to a basic chord, or drop notes. For example, in "Car Chase," which follows, you change the A to Aadd9 by "unfretting" the second string (dropping a note); then you fret the second string one fret higher than usual to make an A suspended (an add-on).

Dropping a note

Adding onto a chord

"Car Chase" has a groove reminiscent of Tracy Chapman's "Fast Car," or "Blue Nancy." The backup picking features drop-offs and add-ons.

◆21 CAR CHASE

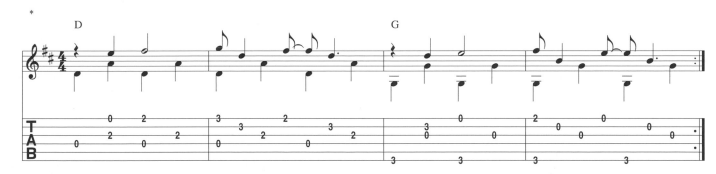

"Birdcalls" is another example of fingerpicking with add-ons and drop-offs, set to a rock groove like that of the Byrds' "Turn, Turn, Turn," and "Mr. Tambourine Man," or any number of Tom Petty hits.

◆22 BIRDCALLS

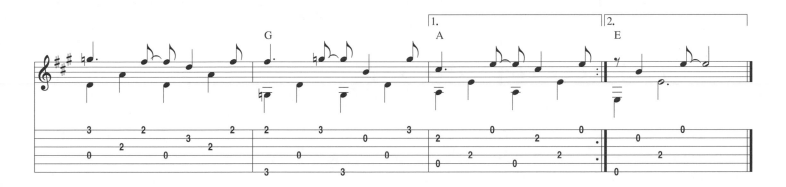

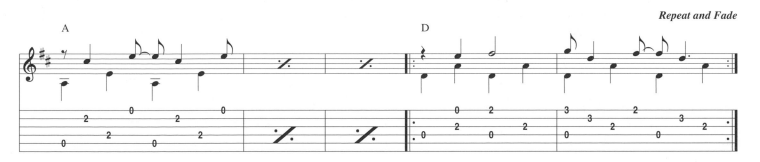

* There is a two-beat pick-up.

Hammer-Ons

Hammering-on is sounding a note with your left hand (instead of picking it with your right hand) by fretting it suddenly. Hammer-ons can be incorporated into fingerpicking patterns, as in "Jagged Iron," which has a funky rhythmic groove similar to Alanis Morissette's "Irony," the Beatles' "She Came In Through the Bathroom Window" and Jimi Hendrix's "Hey Joe."

"Jagged Iron" is in "drop D" tuning, which many fingerpickers use when playing in the key of D: the low E (6th) string is tuned down to D. This gives you a low D bass note, and it changes your G chord:

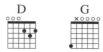

To tune the 6th string down to D, match it with the open 4th (D) string. When it's tuned to D, fret it at the 7th fret to match the open 5th (A) string.

◆23 JAGGED IRON

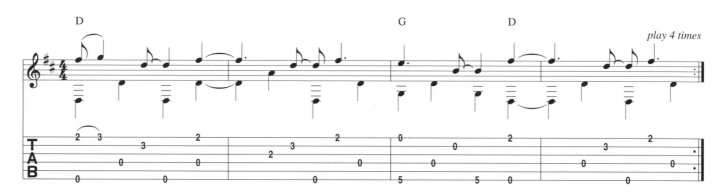

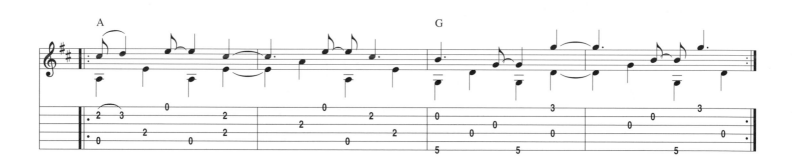

The fingerpicking pattern to "Rocky Roads" includes hammering-on. The tune has the same country-rock groove as Mary-Chapin Carpenter's "Stones in the Road," or the Eagles' "Tequila Sunrise" and "Take it Easy."

24 ROCKY ROADS

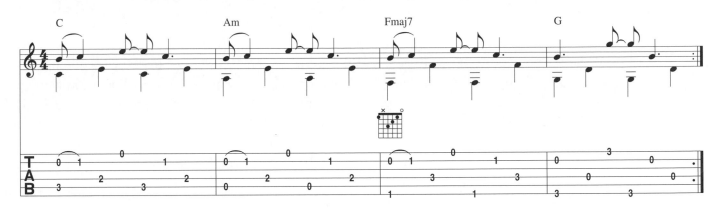

FINGERPICKING SOLOS

So far, you've used your fingers to "fill out the rhythm" on the treble strings, while picking backup patterns. In this chapter, you'll start playing melodies with your fingers. How do you find the melody notes? It's easy if you're familiar with first position scales. Here are the scales and a tune for each of the first-position keys: C, G, D, A and E.

The Key of C: "Will the Circle Be Unbroken"

The Carter Family made this old Southern hymn famous; it has become a country music anthem. It's easy to play in the key of C, when you know the C major scale.

The C Major Scale

Since you'll seldom pick notes lower than the 3rd string with your fingers, this C scale only uses the top three strings. As a result, it's not a full octave. Play it over and over, as written, with your fingers:

Here's an exercise that will help familiarize you with the C scale. It can be played descending (as written) or ascending (backwards). Learn it both ways*:

Playing the Melody

Play the melody to "Circle," with your fingers, until you can do it without reading. Even though you're not picking or strumming chords, fret the appropriate chords with your left hand while playing melody.

*This exercise and all the scale exercises that follow can be played ascending (forward) and descending (backward).

WILL THE CIRCLE BE UNBROKEN

Just the Melody

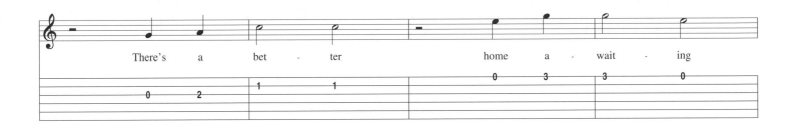

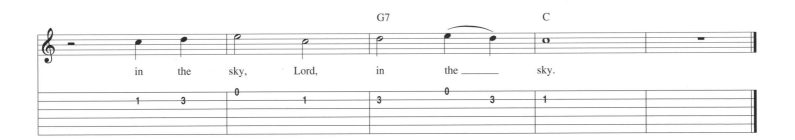

Adding the Alternating Bass

Once you're familiar with the melody, play the arrangement that follows, which combines the melody with the alternating thumb/bass. If you get tangled up playing the melody and thumb/bass at the same time, *don't give up!* Slow down and take a few bars at a time, until you've memorized the piece. Once you learn a few tunes, it gets easier and easier to combine the melody with the bass. Your right hand eventually learns all the rhythmic combinations of thumb and finger, and the thumb/bass becomes automatic. But there's no substitute for memorizing several arrangements like the ones that follow.

WILL THE CIRCLE BE UNBROKEN

Melody and Bass

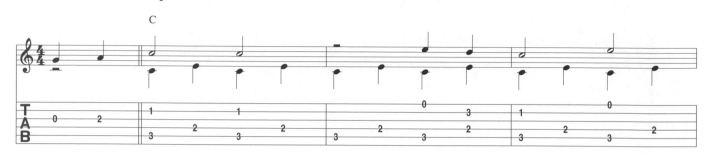

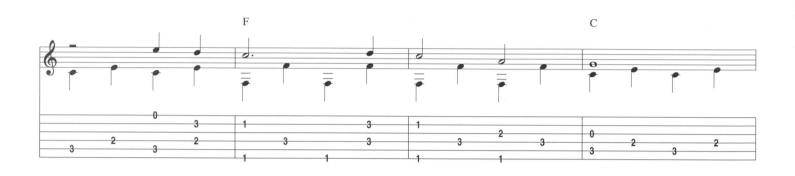

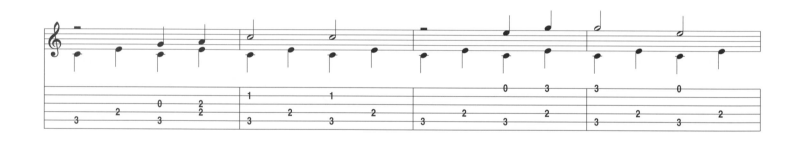

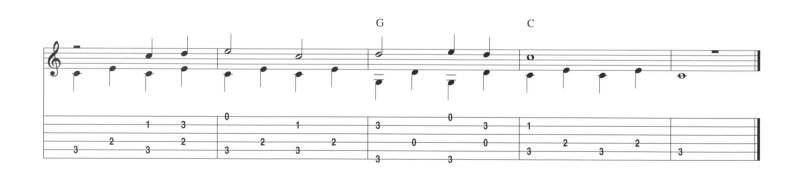

Syncopating the Melody

In the previous arrangement, all the melody notes coincide with bass notes. But the tune doesn't really start to rock until you play some melody notes *between* the bass notes. This makes a much more syncopated, musical rhythmic feel. Try this arrangement.

WILL THE CIRCLE BE UNBROKEN

With Syncopation

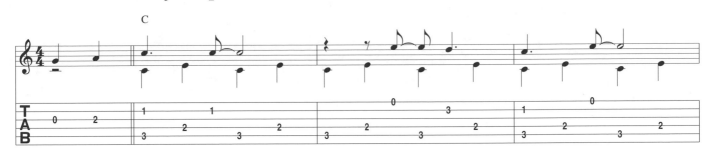

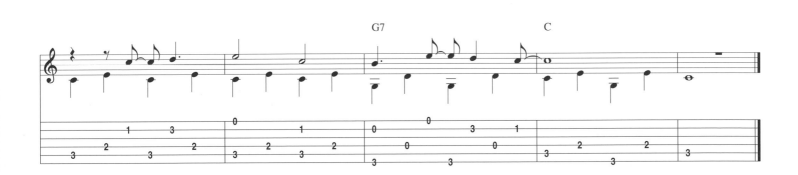

The Key of E: "The Midnight Special"

You'll seldom pick notes lower than the open third string with your fingers, but here's the E major scale from the 4th string/2nd fret, which is an E note.

The E Major Scale

Practice playing "up and down" the scale, as written. Then play this scale exercise:

Playing the Melody

Now play the melody (with your fingers) to the folk/blues tune "The Midnight Special," a prison song about a train that passes by at midnight. It includes one "blue note" (G natural) that is not part of the E major scale:

30 THE MIDNIGHT SPECIAL
Just the Melody

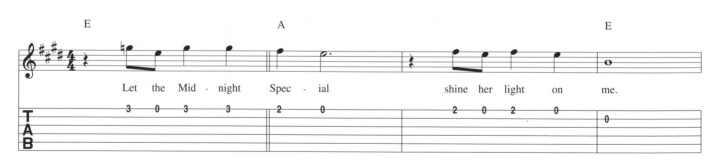

Adding the Alternating Bass

Now add the thumb/bass. Because some of the melody notes in "The Midnight Special" are eighth notes, they fall between the bass notes, so there's built-in syncopation.

⬥31 THE MIDNIGHT SPECIAL
Melody and Bass

Syncopating the Melody

Placing just a few more melody notes between the quarter-note alternating bass makes the tune sound even better:

⬥32 THE MIDNIGHT SPECIAL
With Syncopation

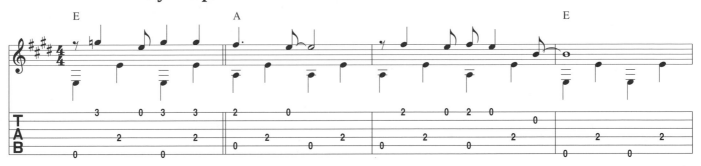

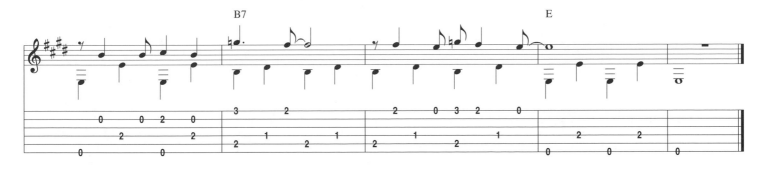

27

The Key of G—"Wabash Blues"

If the G major scale seems familiar when you practice it, that's because it consists of the same notes as the C major scale, with one exception: the F is sharp (up one fret).

The G Major Scale

 Once you've played the G scale a few dozen times, play this scale exercise:

Playing the Melody

"Wabash Blues" is an old Tin Pan Alley song. It has a few chords that may be unfamiliar, including two unusual ways of playing a D7. One is a C7, raised up two frets, the other changes easily from a D to a D7:

To become comfortable with these chords, fret them while playing the melody.

WABASH BLUES
Just the Melody

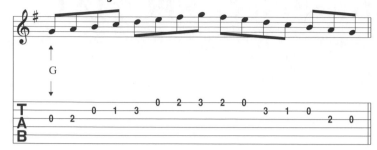

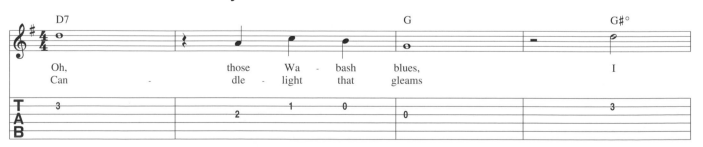

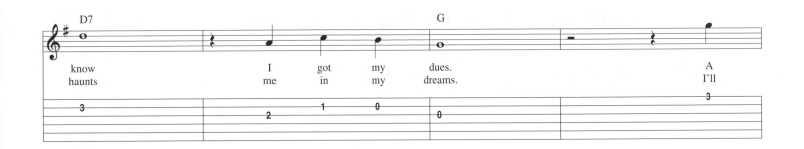

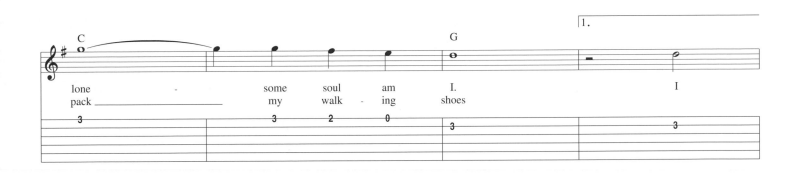

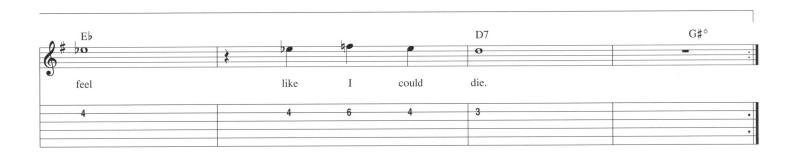

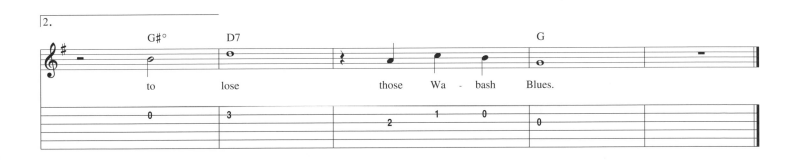

35 WABASH BLUES

Melody and Bass

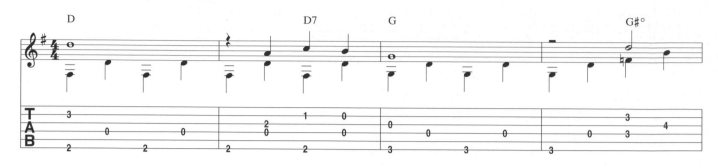

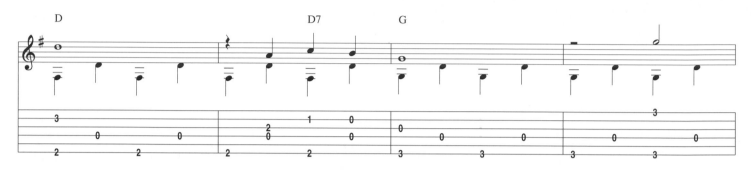

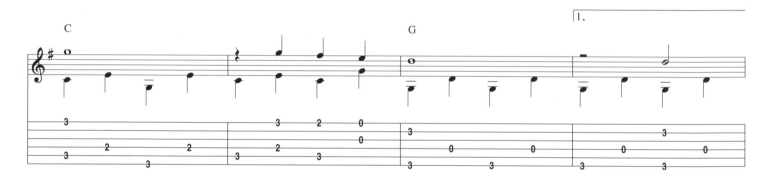

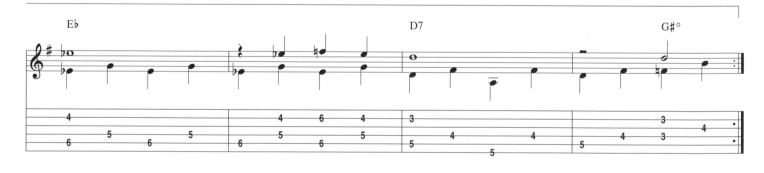

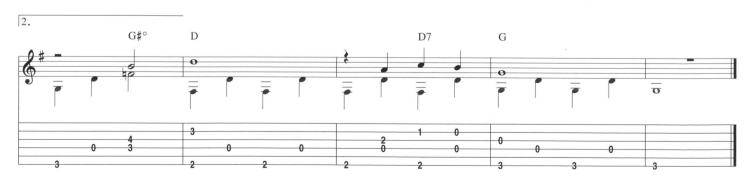

36 WABASH BLUES

With Syncopation

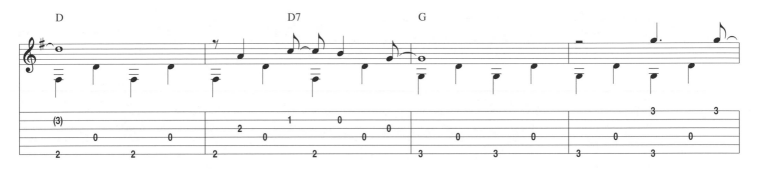

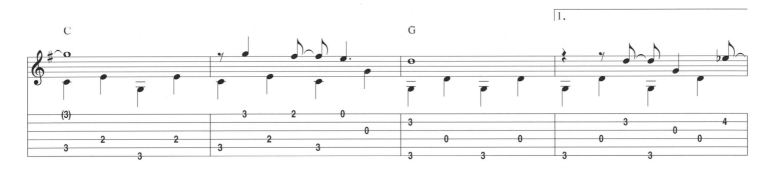

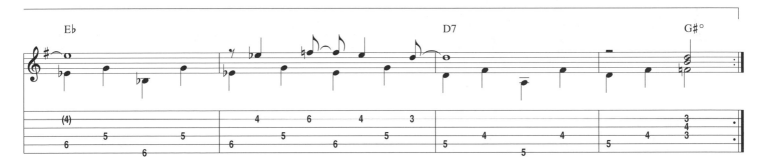

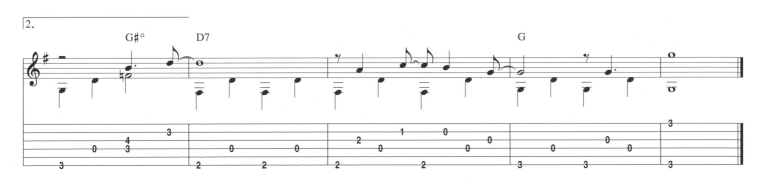

The Key of D—"Stagolee"

The D major scale is the same as the G major scale with a C# instead of C natural. Here's the D major scale and exercise:

The D Major Scale

Playing the Melody

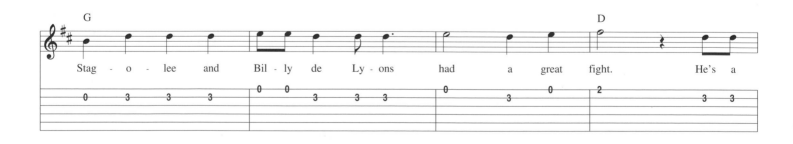

STAGOLEE
Just the Melody

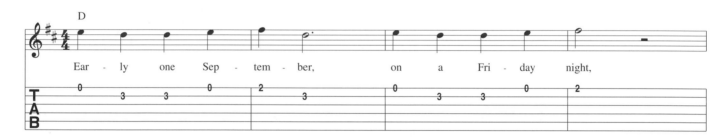

Ear - ly one Sep - tem - ber, on a Fri - day night,

Stag - o - lee and Bil - ly de Ly - ons had a great fight. He's a

bad   man,   that   cru - el   Stag - o - lee.

Adding the Alternating Bass

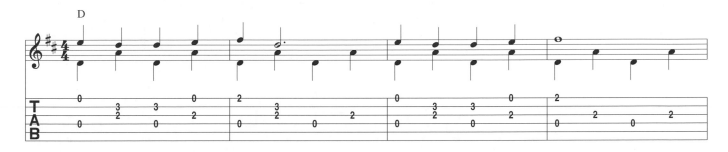

STAGOLEE
Melody and Bass

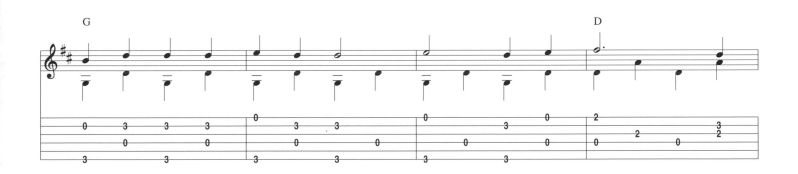

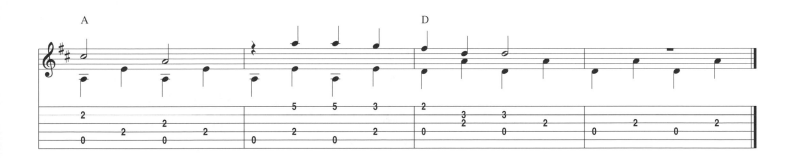

Syncopating the Melody

This syncopated arrangement of "Stagolee" shows how hammer-ons and slides can ornament a melody.

40 STAGOLEE
With Syncopation

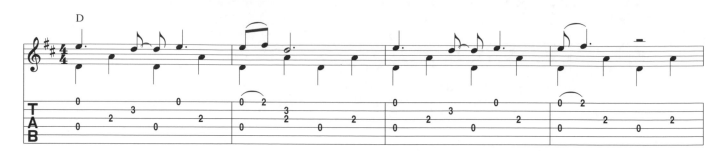

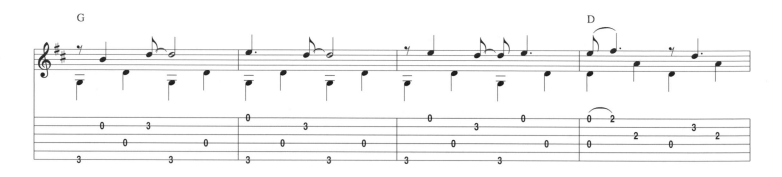

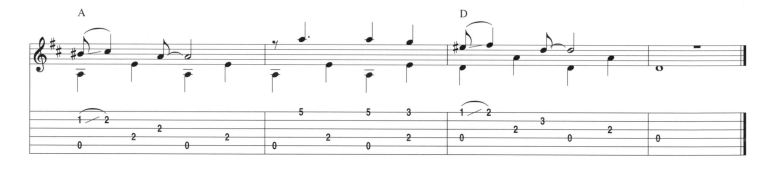

The Key of A—"Hesitation Blues"

This ragtimey blues goes back to the 1920s. It has been recorded by many blues, jazz, country and rock singers, including Reverend Gary Davis, Doc Watson, Jorma Kaukonen and Louis Armstrong. For this version, you need to acquaint yourself with the A major scale, which is the same as the E major scale except for a D natural.

The A Major Scale

Here's the A major scale exercise:

Playing the Melody

"Hesitation Blues" ' melody has two blue notes: C natural and E♭. This arrangement uses the D chord you played in "Wabash Blues."

HESITATION BLUES
Just the Melody

Stand-in' on the cor-ner with a dol-lar in my hand, look-in' for a wom-an who's

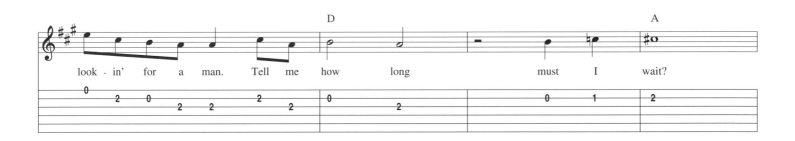

look-in' for a man. Tell me how long must I wait?

Can I get you now, or must I hes-i-tate?

HESITATION BLUES

Melody and Bass

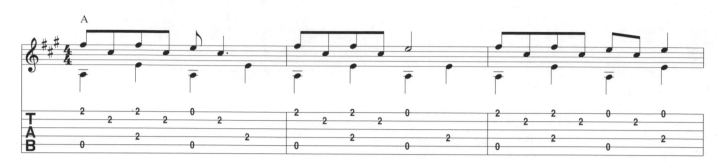

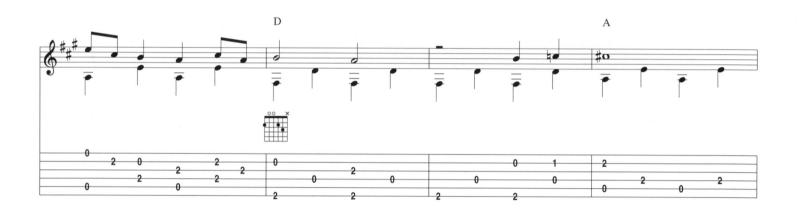

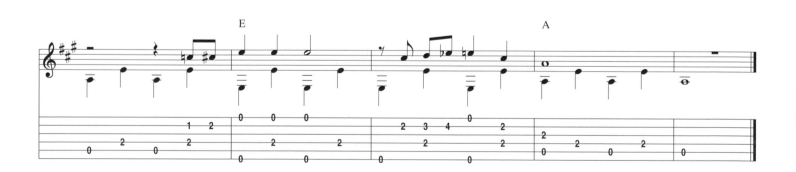

◆44 HESITATION BLUES
With Syncopation

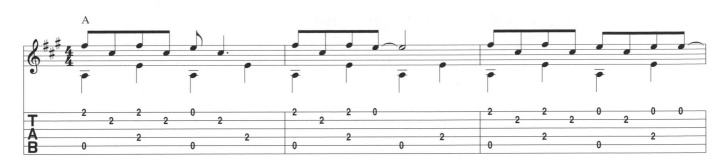

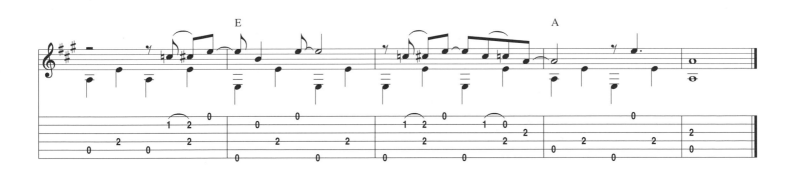

OTHER TEMPOS AND TECHNIQUES

Texas Style, Non-Alternating Bass

In the Texas blues fingerpicking tradition, ruled by luminaries like Lightnin' Hopkins and Mance Lipscomb, the thumb thumps out a steady bass, four beats to the bar, on one note (usually the root of the chord being played), while the fingers pick melody. To accompany singing, you keep the thumb/bass going and play fills with the fingers during pauses in the vocal. This arrangement of the old blues, "See See Rider," is a typical example.

45 SEE SEE RIDER
Backup and Solo

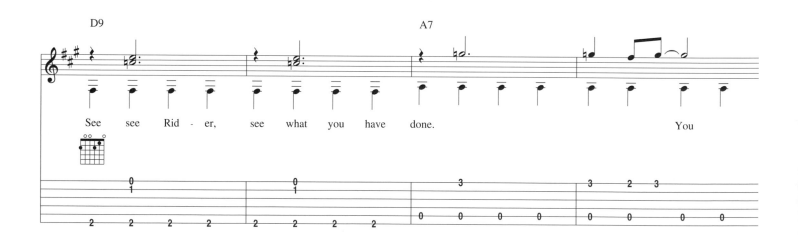

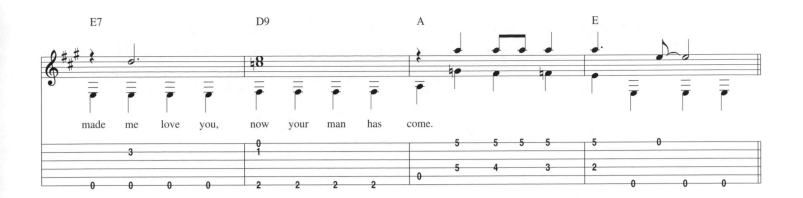

made me love you, now your man has come.

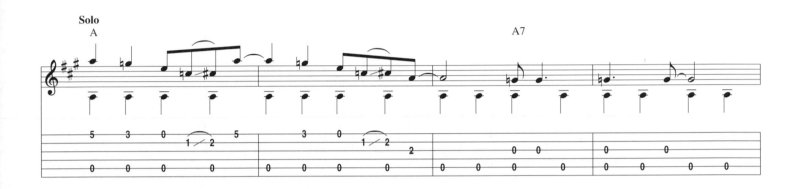

Solo

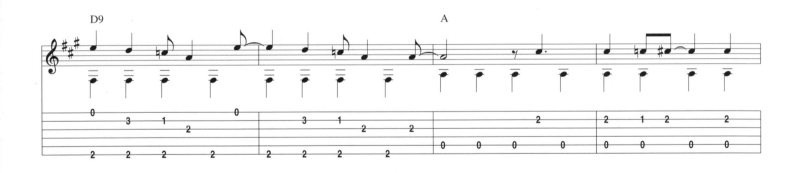

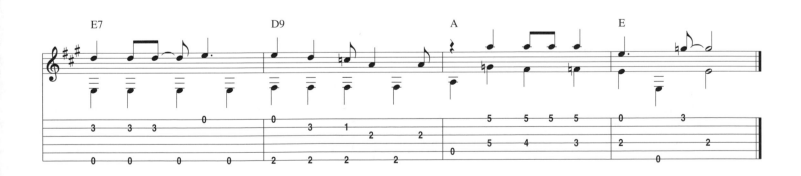

Boogie Bass Lines

This arrangement of See See Rider," in the key of G, includes a backup technique that's used in blues, rock, country and pop music called the boogie bass. The thumb picks a bass line while the index or middle finger fills with a treble string or two, between each bass note.

Here are the boogie bass patterns for the G, C and D chords:

On the recording, the boogie bass lines are played for backup throughout the vocal, as written below. They are also used as fills in the solo, during pauses in the melody.

SEE SEE RIDER
Backup in G

means "repeat the two previous bars"

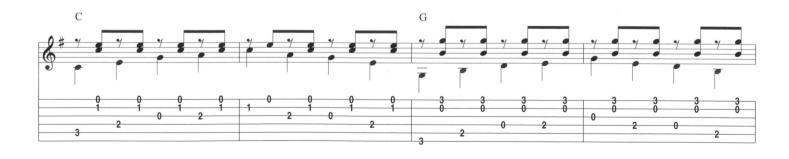

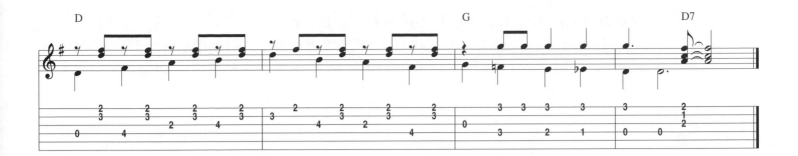

"Stagolee—Backup in E" uses boogie bass patterns for E, A and B7. It includes one-bar and two-bar patterns for the E and A chords.

◆48 STAGOLEE
Backup in E

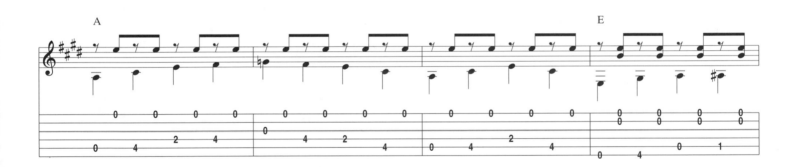

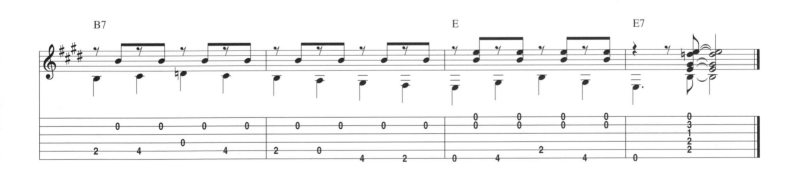

Four-Finger Picking for Rock Ballads

"Unplugged" features a four-finger picking style (actually it's three fingers and thumb) often used in rock ballads like Eric Clapton's "Tears In Heaven." It has the same rhythm groove as "Let It Be Me" by the Everly Brothers and "I'll Be There" by the Jackson Five. Two basic patterns alternate throughout the tune:

50 UNPLUGGED

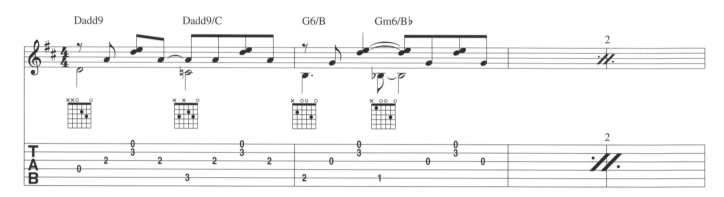

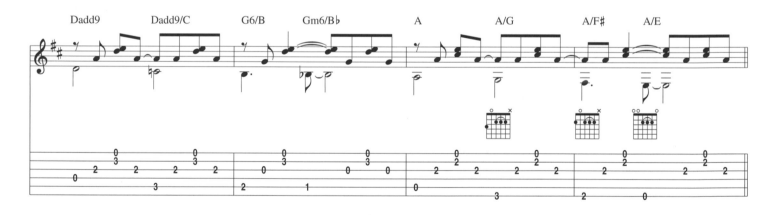

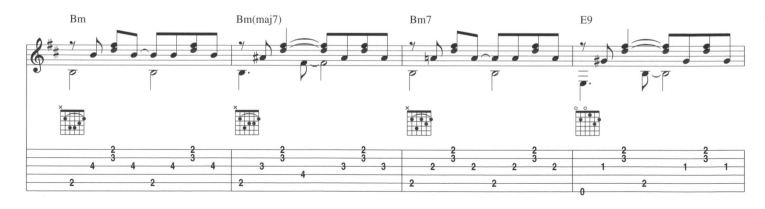

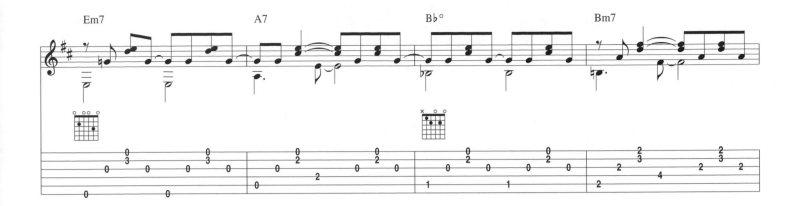

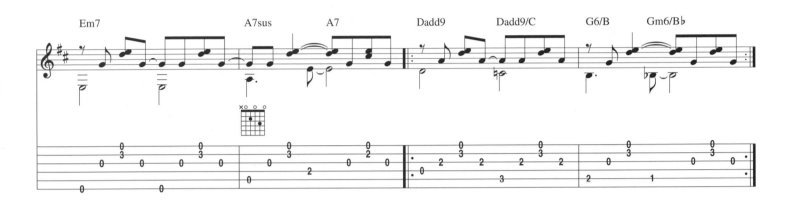

Once you've played "Unplugged" as written, try playing along with the recording using these alternate four- and three-finger patterns:

T I M R M I T R   T I M T I M T M

Waltzes

Since the old cowboy lament, "Streets of Laredo" is in 3/4 time, this rhythmic backup pattern has a "one-two-three" count. It makes use of the ring (third) finger, and it's in "drop D" tuning.

 D   G   Em   Bm

Backup Pattern

T I R I R I T I R I R I
  M   M   M   M

53 STREETS OF LAREDO

Backup

As   I   walked   out   in   the   streets   of   La -
  spied   a   young   cow - boy   all   wrapped   in   white

re - do,   as   I   walked   out   in   La - re - do   one
lin - en,   wrapped   in   white   lin - en   as

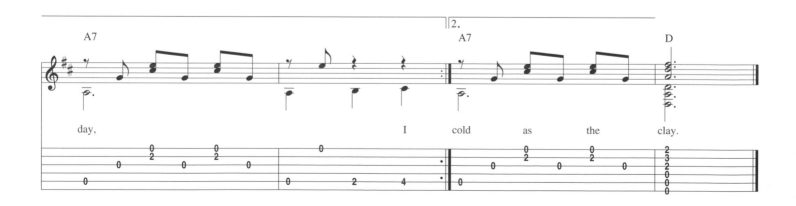

day,   I   cold   as   the   clay.

There's no repetitious pattern in this melodic solo to "Streets of Laredo," but the thumb keeps a "one-two-three" bass pattern going throughout.

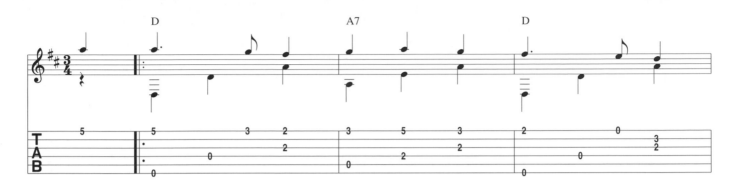

STREETS OF LAREDO
Melodic Solo

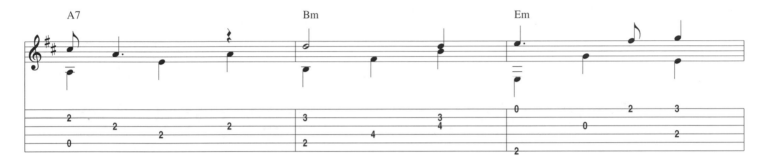

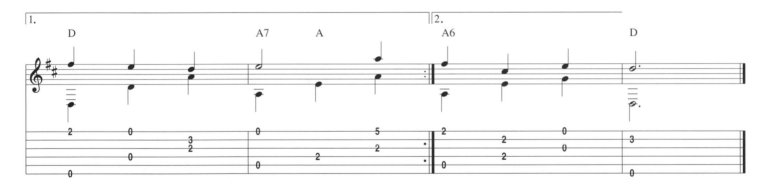

Slower Waltz

"Scarborough Fair" has a slower, less bouncy waltz feel than "Laredo." Here's a backup pattern that creates the rhythmic feel, followed by a backup part for the tune and a solo. As in the solo to "Laredo," the fingers pick melody while the thumb and fingers fill out the rhythm.

Pattern

56 SCARBOROUGH FAIR

Backup and Solo

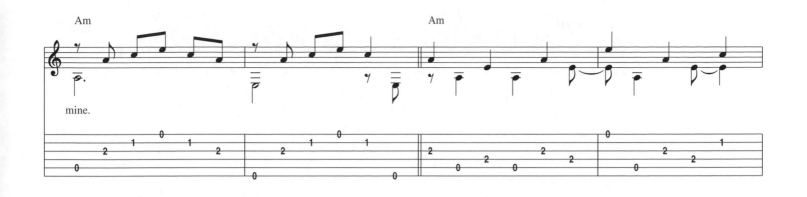

mine.

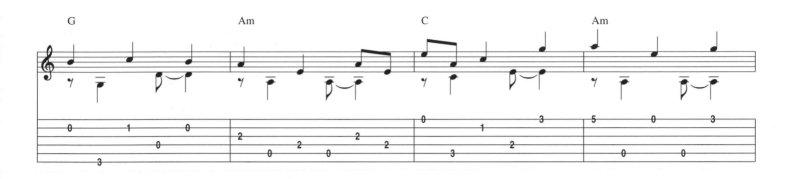

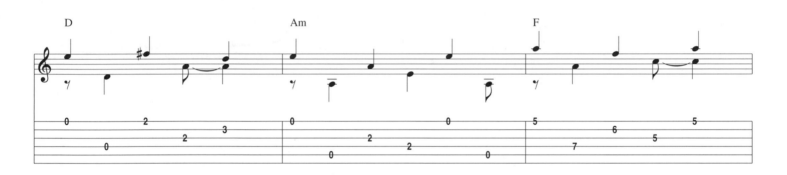

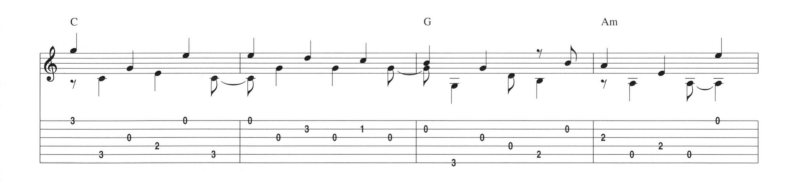

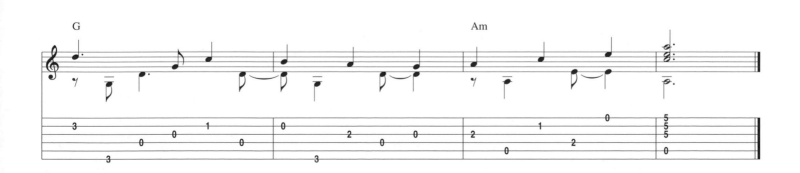

6/8 Time

The "Scarborough Fair" arpeggio pattern works for songs in 6/8, like "Time Is on My Side" (Wilson Pickett, the Rolling Stones), "You Send Me" (Sam Cooke), "This Boy" and "Oh Darling" (the Beatles), "When a Man Loves a Woman" (Percy Sledge) "Tell It Like It Is" (Aaron Neville) and all the '50s ballads like "Oh Donna" and "Sixteen Candles." The old folk/blues "House of the Rising Sun," can be played with this groove:

57 HOUSE OF THE RISING SUN

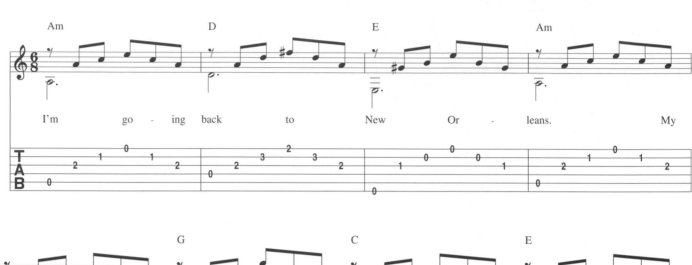

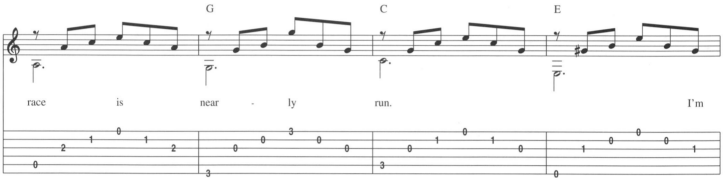

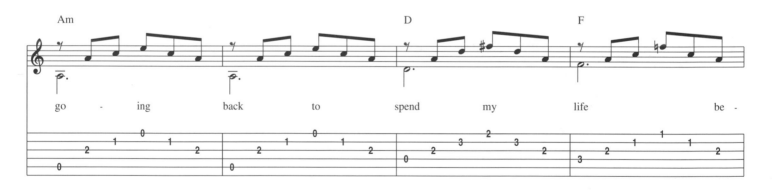